CHINESE
WISDOM

中国智慧

CHINESE WISDOM

Inspiring Quotes on Life, Love and Family

JAMES TRAPP

Copyright © 2025 Amber Books Ltd

Amber Books Ltd
United House
North Road
London N7 9DP
United Kingdom
www.amberbooks.co.uk
Facebook: amberbooks
YouTube: amberbooksltd
Instagram: amberbooksltd
X(Twitter): @amberbooks

All rights reserved. No part of this work may be reproduced, stored in a retrieval system, or transmitted in any form or by any means, electronic, mechanical, photocopying, recording, or otherwise, without the prior permission of the copyright holder.

ISBN: 978-1-83886-520-7

Design & Editorial: Amber Books Ltd

Printed and bound in China

TRADITIONAL CHINESE BOOKBINDING
This book has been produced using traditional Chinese bookbinding techniques, using a method that was developed during the Ming Dynasty (1368–1644) and remained in use until the adoption of Western binding techniques in the early 1900s. In traditional Chinese binding, single sheets of paper are printed on one side only, and each sheet is folded in half, with the printed pages on the outside. The book block is then sandwiched between two boards and sewn together through punched holes close to the cut edges of the folded sheets.

Contents

INTRODUCTION	6
FAMILY	8
LEARNING AND EDUCATION	20
WORK AND BUSINESS	34
VIRTUE AND KINDNESS	46
LOVE AND EMOTION	58
STRATEGY AND AVOIDING CONFLICT	70
CLEAR THINKING	82
PICTURE CREDITS	96

Introduction

Everyone has heard, if not used, the jocular introduction to a piece of supposedly Chinese wisdom: "Confucius, he say…". It will come as no surprise that 99 per cent of these have nothing to do with Confucius and the majority are probably not even Chinese. Even the genuine quotation: "A journey of 1,000 miles begins with a single step" does not come from the writings of Confucius but from *Daodejing* or *Tao Te Ching*, attributed to the sage, Laozi. However, in this volume you will find that a lot of the entries do indeed come from *The Analects* or *Lunyu* of Confucius.

Of course, this should come as no surprise, since the teachings of Confucius, who lived from 551–479 BCE, have been pivotal to Chinese political and social life for more than two millennia

INTRODUCTION

and are front and centre again now in the 21st century. China's reverence and respect for its own cultural and literary traditions mean that while some of the other quotes come under the catch-all attribution 'traditional', many of them come from centuries old poetry, prose and historical works that are still taught in Chinese schools today.

The reader will notice that in quite a few instances, the length of the translation rather exceeds the length of the original quotation. This is partly down to the way the Chinese language functions without the extra definite and indefinite articles, auxiliary verbs and prepositions with which English refines meaning. Equally, if not more important, though, is the extraordinary nature of Chinese characters which, rather than conveying single meanings, encapsulate whole concepts and refine their use by context and combination. So, when dipping into this volume, please take time to enjoy and wonder at the beauty and expressive power of the characters, which are here reproduced in their full, traditional form.

FAMILY

家和萬事興

When a family is in harmony,
it flourishes in 10,000 ways.

– *Anonymous*

FAMILY

家家的鍋子有黑污

Every family's wok has a black patch.

– *Traditional*

FAMILY

家書抵萬金

A letter from home is worth
10,000 gold coins.

– *Du Fu, poet (712–770 CE)*

FAMILY

成家容易養家難

Establishing a household is easy,
feeding it is hard.

– *Traditional*

FAMILY

國有國法家有家規

A country has its laws and
a family has its rules.

– *Ma Feng (20th century CE)*

FAMILY

人不嫌母丑,
狗不嫌家贫

A son does not despise his mother's ugliness,
a dog does not despise its home's poverty.

– *from* Virtuous Writings of the Past: a Ming Dynasty Primer
for Children *(14th–17th century)*

FAMILY

父母的心在儿女，
儿女的心在外頭

Parents' thoughts are on their children,
their children's thoughts are on
the outside world.

– *Traditional*

FAMILY

互相信任才算好伙伴，互相關心才算幸福的家庭

Trusting each other is what makes a good partner,
caring for each other is what makes a happy family.

– Traditional

FAMILY

树大分枝,
人大分家

When a tree grows up, it branches out;
when children grow up, they form their own families.

– Traditional

FAMILY

儿多母苦，
鹽多菜苦

Too many children make a mother suffer,
too much salt makes vegetables bitter.

– Traditional

FAMILY

出門看天色,
進門看色

When you leave your house, look at the sky; when you go home look at your family's expressions.

– *Traditional*

FAMILY

人生就彷彿是一次旅程，不管未來我們會往哪個方向漂泊，最終還是會回到讓我們感覺溫暖的家。家對於我們而言就是一個避風港，家同樣也是將我們從黑暗帶領到光明的'指向塔。

Life is like a journey: no matter which direction we drift in the future, we will eventually return to the home that makes us feel warm. Home is a safe haven for us, and it is also a 'signal tower' that leads us from darkness to light.

– Anonymous

LEARNING AND EDUCATION

有教无類

Teaching does not discriminate.

– *from* Lunyu *or* The Analects, *Confucius (551–479 BCE)*

LEARNING AND EDUCATION

學而不思則罔, 思而不學則殆

To learn without thinking is confusing,
to think without learning is dangerous.

– *from* Lunyu *or* The Analects, *Confucius (551–479 BCE)*

LEARNING AND EDUCATION

子以四教：
文、行、忠、信

Confucius teaches four things:
literature, conduct, loyalty and good faith.

– *from* Lunyu *or* The Analects, *Confucius (551–479 BCE)*

LEARNING AND EDUCATION

學好三年，
學壞三天

It takes three years to learn good habits
but only three days to learn bad ones.

– Traditional

LEARNING AND EDUCATION

學如逆水行舟，
不進則退

Learning is like rowing against the current:
if you don't progress, you go backwards.

– *Gu Yanwu, political philosopher (1613–1682)*

LEARNING AND EDUCATION

知之者不如好之者,
好之者不如乐之者

Wanting to learn is more important than knowing how to learn; loving learning is more important than wanting to learn.

– *from* Lunyu *or* The Analects, *Confucius (551–479 BCE)*

LEARNING AND EDUCATION

学然后知不足

To learn is to encounter one's own ignorance.

– Book of Rites *(5th–1st century BCE)*

LEARNING AND EDUCATION

学如登山

Learning is like climbing a mountain.

– *Xu Gan, philosopher and poet (170–217 CE)*

LEARNING AND EDUCATION

读万卷书行万里路

Read many books, travel many roads.

– *Dong Qichang, artist and calligrapher (1555–1636 CE)*

LEARNING AND EDUCATION

活到老，学到老

Live into old age; study into old age.

– *Traditional*

LEARNING AND EDUCATION

我们要能够做，做的最高境界就是创造。只知学而不知做，就不是真的教育。有行动之勇敢，才有真知的收获

We must be able to do, and the highest level of doing is creation. If we only know how to learn but not how to do, it is not true education. Only with the courage to act can we gain true knowledge.

– *Tao Xingzhi, educator and academic (1891–1946)*

LEARNING AND EDUCATION

教育植根於愛

Education is rooted in love.

– *Lu Xun, short story writer, translator and literary critic (1881–1936)*

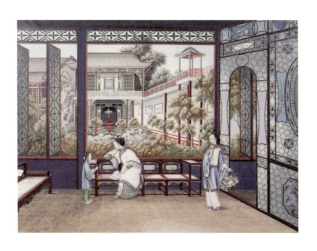

LEARNING AND EDUCATION

少年易老學難成，
一寸光陰不可輕。
未覺池塘春草夢，
階前梧葉已秋聲。

Youth fades easily and learning is hard to achieve;
no moment of time should be taken lightly.
Before you realise that the spring grass in the pond
is now only a dream, the leaves of the parasol tree
in front of the steps are already making autumn sounds.

– Zhu Xi, philosopher, poet and politician (1130–1200)

LEARNING AND EDUCATION

WORK AND BUSINESS

從沒有白費的努力，也沒有碰巧的成功

There is no such thing as wasted effort
or accidental success.

– Traditional

WORK AND BUSINESS

沒有傘的孩子，
必須努力奔跑

Children without umbrellas have to run hard.

– *Meng Haoran, poet (died 740 CE)*

WORK AND BUSINESS

一絲不苟

Always be meticulous in following the rules.
Literal meaning: not one loose thread.

– *Traditional*

WORK AND BUSINESS

工欲善其事，
必先利其器

If you want to do good work,
you must always sharpen your tools.

– *from* Lunyu *or* The Analects, *Confucius (551–479 BCE)*

WORK AND BUSINESS

人無遠慮，必有近憂

If you don't plan for the future,
you will soon have problems now.

– *from* Lunyu *or* The Analects, *Confucius (551–479 BCE)*

WORK AND BUSINESS

先行其言，而後從之

Say what you have to say, then follow up on it.

– *from* Lunyu *or* The Analects, *Confucius (551–479 BCE)*

WORK AND BUSINESS

朽木不可雕也

You can't carve rotten wood.

– *from* Lunyu *or* The Analects, *Confucius (551–479 BCE)*

WORK AND BUSINESS

過而不改，是謂過矣

If you do not correct your mistakes,
you are still making mistakes.

– *from* Lunyu *or* The Analects, *Confucius (551–479 BCE)*

WORK AND BUSINESS

失败是成功之母

Failure is the mother of success.

– *Traditional*

WORK AND BUSINESS

一日之計在於晨

A day's planning starts at dawn.

– *Song Ruozhao, poet and scholar (761–828 CE)*

WORK AND BUSINESS

靠山山會倒,
靠水水會流,
靠自己永遠不倒

Mountains may collapse and water may flow away
if you rely on them, but you will never be let down
if you rely on yourself.

– *Anonymous*

WORK AND BUSINESS

挫折時，要像大樹一樣，被砍了，
還能再長；也要像雜草一樣，雖讓
人踐踏，但還能勇敢地活下去

When you encounter setbacks, you should be like
a big tree, which can grow again after being cut down;
you should also be like weeds, which can bravely survive
even though they are trampled on.

– Anonymous

VIRTUE AND KINDNESS

己所不欲，勿施于人

Don't do to others what you would not want done to you.

– *from* Lunyu *or* The Analects, *Confucius (551–479 BCE)*

VIRTUE AND KINDNESS

勿以善小而不為,
勿以惡小而為之。

Do not ignore small kindnesses done to you and
do not inflict small cruelties on others.

– *Liu Bei, Shu Han Dynasty founder (161–223 CE)*

VIRTUE AND KINDNESS

以柔克剛

Overcome firmness with flexibility.

– *Zhuge Liang, statesman and strategist (181–234 CE)*

VIRTUE AND KINDNESS

节制其欲，而不失其真

Control your desires without losing your true self.

– *from* Shi Ji *or* Records of the Grand Historian, *Sima Qian*
(145–86 BCE)

VIRTUE AND KINDNESS

大音希聲，大象無形

Great sounds are silent; great images are invisible.

– *from* Daodejing, *Laozi (circa 5th century BCE)*

VIRTUE AND KINDNESS

有德者必有言，
有言者不必有德

The virtuous man must speak out,
but not everyone who speaks out is virtuous.

– *from* Lunyu *or* The Analects, *Confucius (551–479 BCE)*

VIRTUE AND KINDNESS

静以修身，俭以养德

Be quiet to cultivate yourself, and be frugal to cultivate virtue.

– *Zhuge Liang, statesman and strategist (181–234 CE)*

VIRTUE AND KINDNESS

不患位之不尊，而患德之不崇；不耻禄之不伙，而耻智之不博

Don't worry about your low position, but think about whether your morals are perfect; don't feel ashamed that your income is not high enough, but think about whether your knowledge is profound enough.

– *Zhang Heng, scientist and statesman (78–139 CE)*

VIRTUE AND KINDNESS

芝兰生于深林,不以无人而不芳

The orchid grows in the deep forest and does not lose its fragrance if there is no one there.

– *from* Lunyu *or* The Analects, *Confucius (551–479 BCE)*

VIRTUE AND KINDNESS

心如明镜台，
时时勤拂拭

The heart is like a mirror; always keep it clean.

– *Yuquan Shenxiu, monk and Chan master (606–706 CE)*

VIRTUE AND KINDNESS

鋤一惡，長十善

Eliminate one evil, and you will develop ten virtues.

– *from* History of the Song Dynasty: Vol 281 *(completed 1343)*

VIRTUE AND KINDNESS

善心生，亦惟劳乃乐也

A kind heart is born but only hard work
can bring happiness.

– *Yun Daiying, politician (1895–1931)*

LOVE AND EMOTION

愛親做親

Loving families make for good in-laws.

– *Traditional*

LOVE AND EMOTION

兩情若是長久時，又豈在朝朝暮暮？

If our love is forever, why should we be together day and night?

– *Qin Guan, Song Dynasty poet (1049–1100)*

LOVE AND EMOTION

不亂於心，不困於情，
不畏將來，不念過往，
如此，安好

Don't be confused in your heart, don't be trapped in your emotions, don't fear the future, don't think about the past, so you will be at peace.

– Feng Zikai, artist (1898–1975)

LOVE AND EMOTION

直道相思了無益，
未妨惆悵是清狂

Although it is useless to miss someone, it is not a problem to be a bit sad and crazy.

– *Li Shangyin, Tang Dynasty poet and politician (813–858 CE)*

LOVE AND EMOTION

易求無價寶，
難得有心郎

It is easy to find priceless treasures,
but hard to find a loving man.

– *Yu Xuanji, Tang Dynasty poet (844–871 CE)*

LOVE AND EMOTION

情之所鍾，雖醜不嫌

If you love someone, you won't despise them
even if they are ugly.

– *Shen Fu, Qing Dynasty private secretary and autobiographer
(1763–circa 1825)*

LOVE AND EMOTION

庭有枇杷樹，吾妻死之年所手植也，今已亭亭如蓋矣

There is a loquat tree in the yard, which was planted by my wife in the year she died. Now it has grown tall and majestic like a canopy.

– *Gui Youguang, Ming Dynasty writer (1506–1571)*

LOVE AND EMOTION

相思似海深,
舊事如天遠

Longing is as deep as the sea, and old memories are as far as the sky.

– *Le Wan, Song Dynasty courtesan (dates unknown)*

LOVE AND EMOTION

老來多健忘,
唯不忘相思

People often forget things as they grow old, but they never forget their love.

– *Bai Juyi, Tang Dynasty poet (772–846 CE)*

LOVE AND EMOTION

挑兮達兮、在城闕兮。
一日不見、如三月兮

To and fro I pace on the high city walls; one day without you is like three whole months.

– Book of Songs *(12th–7th century BCE)*

LOVE AND EMOTION

长相知，才能不相疑；
不相疑，才能长相知

Only when we know each other for a long time can we stop doubting each other; only when we stop doubting each other can we know each other for a long time.

– Cao Yu, playwright (1910–1996)

LOVE AND EMOTION

相知无远近,
万里尚为邻

Knowing each other is not about distance, and we are still neighbours even if we are thousands of miles apart.

– Zhang Jiuling, Tang Dynasty poet (678–740 CE)

STRATEGY AND AVOIDING CONFLICT

百戰百勝，非善之善者也；不戰而屈人之兵，善之善者也

To win every battle is not the greatest of all skills;
to defeat the enemy without joining battle at all
is the greatest of the great.

– *from* The Art of War, *Sun Tzu (544–496 BCE)*

STRATEGY AND AVOIDING CONFLICT

五指之更彈，不若拳手之一挃；萬人之更替，不如百人之俱至也

The flick of five fingers is not as good as the strike of a fist; the individual replacement of ten thousand people is not as good as the simultaneous arrival of a hundred.

– *from* The Huainanzi, *Liu An (179–122 BCE)*

STRATEGY AND AVOIDING CONFLICT

以寡御衆之道，須聯數人之心爲一心，合數萬人之力爲一體

To control the majority with the minority, one must unite the hearts of several people into one heart and the strength of tens of thousands of people into one body.

– from a collection of the Ming Dynasty's Essays on State Affairs

STRATEGY AND AVOIDING CONFLICT

上兵伐謀

The highest form of warfare is to outthink the enemy.

– *from* The Art of War, *Sun Tzu (544–496 BCE)*

STRATEGY AND AVOIDING CONFLICT

戰不必勝，不苟接刃；
攻不必取，不苟勞衆

If you are not sure of victory in a battle, then do not fight rashly; if you cannot guarantee victory in an attack, then do not mobilise the troops without due consideration.

– *from* The Huainanzi, *Liu An (179–122 BCE)*

STRATEGY AND AVOIDING CONFLICT

用兵人人料必勝者，中即伏敗機；人人料必挫者，中即伏生機

When everyone expects victory, there is the hidden possibility of defeat; when everyone expects defeat, there is the hidden possibility of survival.

– *Zeng Guofan, Qing Dynasty statesman (1811–1872)*

STRATEGY AND AVOIDING CONFLICT

不可勝在己，可勝在敵

You can make yourself invincible, but victory depends on the enemy.

– *from* The Art of War, *Sun Tzu (544–496 BCE)*

STRATEGY AND AVOIDING CONFLICT

爲一身謀則愚. 而爲天下謀則智

To plan for oneself is foolish, but to plan for the world is wise.

– *Su Xun, essayist and philosopher (1009–1066)*

STRATEGY AND AVOIDING CONFLICT

銅山西崩，洛鐘東應

When Mt. Tong collapses in the west,
the Luo Bell rings in the east.
Meaning: great events influence each other.

– Traditional

STRATEGY AND AVOIDING CONFLICT

養兵千日，用兵一時

Maintain troops for a thousand days to deploy
them for a single moment.

– *from* History of the Southern Dynasties *(7th century CE)*

STRATEGY AND AVOIDING CONFLICT

兵者，詭道也，故能而示之
不能，用而示之不用，近而
示之遠，遠而示之近。

The art of war is to use deception; therefore, when one is capable, pretend to be incapable; when one is deploying an attack, pretend not to be; when an attack is close, pretend it is far away; when an attack is far away, pretend it is close.

– *from* The Art of War, *Sun Tzu (544–496 BCE)*

STRATEGY AND AVOIDING CONFLICT

知彼知己，百戰不殆；
不知彼知己，一勝一負，
不知彼不知己，每戰必殆。

If you know yourself and know the enemy, you will not be in danger in a hundred battles. If you know yourself but do not know the enemy, you will only win one battle and lose another. If you know neither yourself nor the enemy, you will be in danger in every battle.

– *from* The Art of War, *Sun Tzu (544–496 BCE)*

CLEAR THINKING

天分高的人如果懶惰成性，亦即不自努力以發展他的才能，則其成就也不會很大，有時反會不如那天分比他低的人

If a person with great talent is lazy, that is, does not work hard to develop his talents, his achievements will not be great, and sometimes he will not be as good as those who are lesser than him.

– *Mao Dun, novelist, playwright, journalist and critic (1896–1981)*

CLEAR THINKING

CLEAR THINKING

事若求全何所樂？

What is the point in seeking perfection?

– *from* The Dream of the Red Chamber, *Cao Xueqin (1710–1765)*

CLEAR THINKING

要知山下路，
須問過來人

If you want to know the way down the mountain,
you must ask someone who has been there.

– *from* Journey to the West, *Wu Cheng'en (1506–1582)*

CLEAR THINKING

老姜辣味大，
老人经验多

Old ginger is spicier, old people have more experience.

– Traditional

CLEAR THINKING

舊書不厭百回讀，熟讀精思子自知蘇軾

I don't get tired of reading old books hundreds of times,
and it is by reading them well, that I know myself.

– *Su Shi, Song Dynasty poet, essayist and statesman (1037–1101)*

CLEAR THINKING

學者先要會疑

Scholars must first know how to doubt.

– *Cheng Yi, Song Dynasty philosopher and essayist (1033–1107)*

CLEAR THINKING

吾生也有涯,
而知也無涯

My life is finite, but knowledge is infinite.

– Zhuangzi (circa 4th century BCE)

CLEAR THINKING

無所不能的人實在一無所能，無所不專的專家實在是一無所專

A man who knows everything can really do nothing;
an expert who knows everything really knows nothing.

– *Zou Taofen, journalist and political activist (1895–1944)*

CLEAR THINKING

知之者不如好之者，
好之者不如樂之者

Those who know are not as good as those who are good,
and those who are good are not as good as those
who are happy.

– *from* Lunyu *or* The Analects, *Confucius (551–479 BCE)*

CLEAR THINKING

非淡泊無以明志,
非寧靜無以致遠

Without indifference, there is no clear ambition;
without serenity, there is no far-reaching goal.

– *Zhuge Liang, statesman and strategist (181–234 CE)*

CLEAR THINKING

知识有如人体血液一样的宝贵。人缺少了血液,
身体就要衰弱,
人缺少了知识, 头脑就要枯竭

Knowledge is as valuable as human blood. If a person lacks blood, his body will be weakened, and if he lacks knowledge, his mind will be exhausted.

– *Gao Shiqi, Qing Dynasty scholar and politician (1645–1703)*

CLEAR THINKING

平日涵養之功，臨事持守之力。涵養、持守之久，則臨事愈益精明。平日養得根本。

The merit of daily cultivation is the power of perseverance in dealing with things. The longer you cultivate yourself and persevere, the more astute you will be in dealing with things. Daily cultivation is the foundation.

– *Zhu Xi, philosopher, poet and politician (1130–1200)*

CLEAR THINKING

Picture Credits

Alamy: 6 (CPA Media), 8 (Historic Illustrations), 11 (Antiqua Print Gallery), 20 (Interfoto), 31 & 33 (The Print Collector), 35 (Heritage Image Partnership), 37 (George Henry Malon), 41 (incamerastock), 42 (CPA Media), 45 (chuck), 47 (Mariano Garcia), 53 (CPA Media), 57 (North Wind Picture Archives), 62 (The Print Collector), 66 & 68 (Heritage Image Partnership), 75 (CPA Media), 76, 77 (CPA Media), 79 (Heritage Image Partnership), 81 (Historic Illustrations), 84 (Album), 87 (View Stock), 89 (charistoone-travel)

Art Institute of Chicago: 19, 22, 50

Dreamstime: 7 (Verdelho), 16 (Galina Drokina), 43 (Xianghong Wu), 72 (Elwoodchu)

Freer Gallery of Art: 26 (Arthur M. Sackler Gallery Archives), 38 (Charles Lang Freer)

Getty Images: 10 (De Agostini), 71 & 74 (Pictures from History), 95 (Heritage Images)

Library of Congress: 80

Los Angeles County Museum of Art: 73, 91

Metropolitan Museum of Art, New York: 5, 9, 12-15, 17, 18, 23, 24, 27-30, 34, 36, 40, 48, 49, 51, 52, 54-56, 58-61, 63, 67, 69, 70, 78, 83, 85, 86, 90, 93

Shutterstock: 44 (Baoyan), 64 (Asharkyu), 65 (Lillian GZ)

Wellcome Foundation: 21, 25, 39, 46, 88, 92